Chae's Guide Book:
How to be the BEST big Brother
or Sister you can be!

By Chae Blount

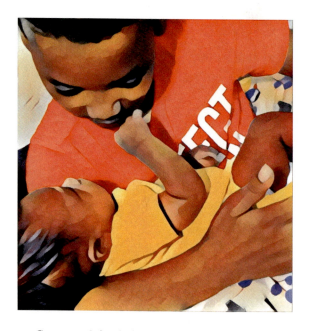

Cover art & book design layout by Dianna Rose
Illustrations & Photography © 2017 Dianna Rose
Contributor: Dianna Rose
Edited by Leila Rose-Gordon and Dawnette Blackwood-Rhoomes
Published by Dianna Rose, Queens, NY.
Printed by CreateSpace, An Amazon.com Company
CreateSpace, Charleston S.C.

All rights reserved. © 2017 Dianna Rose

This is a work of non-fiction.

ISBN-13: 978-1543068764
ISBN-10:1543068766

No part of this book may be reproduced in any form or by any means, stored in any retrieval system, or transmitted in any form or by any means—electronic, mechanical, photocopy, recording, or otherwise—without prior written permission of the publisher, except as provided by United States of America copyright law. For permission requests, reading or booking inquiries write to the publisher, at msdiannarose@gmail.com

To God – to you be all the honor, the glory and the praise!

To my Sethy – you are the best LITTLE brother
in the whole world and I love you very much!
– C. B.

To my Chae Chae and my Little Night Owl Seth,
My purpose and destiny is to be called your Mommy. I love you both to LIFE.
– D. R.

Hi! My name is Chae and I'm a new BIG brother! Having a little brother or sister is a very BIG responsibility and I have learned so much. Now, I want to help by giving you my 10 tips to being the best BIG brother or sister you can be!

#1: Always, always, always wash your hands before you hold or touch your new baby brother or sister.

#2: Mommies get really busy when they have a new born baby. That means you'll have to help out as much as you can. Cleaning up after yourself is a great way to start!

#3: Babies are very little and they cannot help themselves.

So DO NOT put any blankets, pillows or stuffed toys in their cribs.

These things can be very dangerous if it covers their little faces.

#4: Helping to change diapers is NOT an easy job because babies move and wiggle a whole lot. Be sure to have the diapers and wipes near by because it makes changing the baby so much easier.

#5: When your baby brother or sister is really really hungry they'll try to eat your face, so make sure your face is always nice and clean!

#6: Babies need a lot of rest to grow and mommies need rest too!

When the baby falls asleep don't wake the baby up by being too loud.

This is a great time to play quietly so keep your favorite games nearby.

#7: Babies cry for many different reasons and sometimes for no reason at all. You can help to calm the baby down by singing a song or saying your A, B, C's.

#8: Your baby brother or sister will like when you act silly. You should dance around with your hands in the air or make funny faces.

#9: Reading a book is a great way to spend time with the new baby. Read as many books to the baby as you possibly can and be sure to make it lots of fun!

#10: The most IMPORTANT tip of all is to LOVE your baby brother or sister with all your heart!

About the author

Chae Blount is a very active 8 year old boy who loves eating popcorn; ice-cream with whipped cream; playing Minecraft and Roblox; singing on the children's choir at his church; going to his cousin G's house; watching movies with his mommy, and playing with his new baby brother Seth.

Chae is in the third grade and his favorite subjects are math and science. He wants to be a scientist when he grows up. Chae is very generous and caring and tries his best to be a good son, brother and friend. Through his books Chae hopes to inspire children all over the world to love and enjoy reading and to create stories of their own.

Chae's 10 Tips

#1: Always, always, always wash your hands before you hold or touch your new baby brother or sister.

#2: Mommies get really busy when they have a new born baby. That means you'll have to help out as much as you can. Cleaning up after yourself is a great way to start!

#3: Babies are very little and they cannot help themselves. So DO NOT put any blankets, pillows or stuffed toys in their cribs. These things can be very dangerous if it covers their little faces.

#4: Helping to change diapers is NOT an easy job because babies move and wiggle a whole lot. Be sure to have the diapers and wipes near by because it makes changing the baby so much easier.

#5: When your baby brother or sister is really really hungry they"ll try to eat your face, so make sure your face is always nice and clean!

#6: Babies need a lot of rest to grow and mommies need rest too, so when the baby falls asleep don't wake the baby up by being too loud. This is a great time to play quietly so keep your favorite games nearby.

#7: Babies cry for many different reasons and sometimes for no reason at all. You can help to calm the baby down by singing a song or saying your A, B, C's.

#8: Your baby brother or sister will like when you act silly. You should dance around with your hands in the air or make funny faces.

#9: Reading a book is a great way to spend time with the baby. Read as many books to the baby as you possibly can and be sure to make it lots of fun!

#10: The most IMPORTANT tip of all is to LOVE your baby brother or sister with all your heart!

What I have learned about being a BIG _____ is.........

_____

_____

_____

_____

_____

_____

_____

_____

_____

_____

_____

_____

_____

Made in the USA
Middletown, DE
13 April 2017